Little Animal Sermons

Six Children's Sermons With Activity Pages

Julia E. Bland

CSS Publishing Company, Inc., Lima, Ohio

Dedicated to
Wendy, Marcia, Lendi, Petra, and Diana

ISBN: 0-7880-1349-1   PRINTED IN U.S.A.

Table Of Contents

Introduction

Most boys and girls like animals. These six sermons for children take a look at the habits of seven different animals to teach some Bible truths.

The objects or visual aids in this series are the simple pictures of animals found on the coloring page side of the activity sheets. With crayons or markers brightly color a copy of each page. Mount on construction paper to make each page sturdy and attractive. Or use pictures from your library. The sermon "The Dog, Pansy" is handled differently, but simply. These lessons are not limited to morning worship. They may be used any time there is opportunity for Christian education of children.

Suggestions From The Author

Study the sermon so that you can tell it in your own words, using your own personality and with the needs of your local children in mind.

The sermon as given is to get you started. Be open to the Holy Spirit as he guides you to add your own personal observations.

If you need notes, make them small and tuck them inside your Bible at the page where you will be reading the Scripture.

Open the Bible and read from it. Children need to know that what you say really is from the Scriptures.

Ask questions and allow time for the children to answer. This will get them thinking and involved, but children can say unexpected things, so be ready to guide them back to the subject.

Before the worship hour, clip the activity sheet, a pencil, and crayons to a clipboard to be ready to hand to each child when the children's time is over.

As you pray and prepare, claim the Lord's promise in Isaiah 55:11:

So shall my word be that goes out from my mouth;
it shall not return to me empty,
but it shall accomplish that which I purpose,
and succeed in the thing for which I sent it.

May God bless your efforts.

Julia Bland

The Turtle: Sheltered By The Presence Of God

"God is ... a very present help in trouble." — Psalm 46:1

Scripture: Psalm 46:1-2a; John 14:23

Visual Aid: Picture of the box turtle

Handouts: Activity sheets

Advance Preparations: Copy enough activity sheets for each child to have one and have them ready to hand out. Copy and color the picture of the turtle to use as a visual aid as you give the lesson. Or if you prefer, check with your library for pictures to show your children.

The Sermon:

Have you ever seen a turtle? God has made a turtle in a special way. * It has two shells, a rounded one on the top and a rather flat one on the bottom. Its head, legs, and tail stick out between them. If the turtle is afraid or in danger, it pulls its legs, head, and tail in between the two shells and clamps them together. The hard shells give it protection. Turtles have such good protection that many live to be very old, eighty years or so. It's good that they can carry their shelter around with them.

Did you know that God's people carry protection around with them, too? Jesus said in John 14:23 that if anyone will love him and do what he says, then he and the heavenly Father will come to them and make their home with them. We do not see him because he comes as the Holy Spirit, but he has promised to be with us if we love and obey him.

Do you love Jesus? Do you try to do what he wants you to? How do we know what he wants? The Bible tells us. If you do love Jesus and try to obey him, then he is with you. Listen to what the Bible says in Psalm 46:1 and part of verse 2: "God is our refuge [that means shelter] and strength, a very present help in trouble. Therefore we will not fear."

Jesus is *a very present help in trouble.* Isn't he a wonderful Lord?

*Use visual aid

The Dog, Pansy: Sheltered By God's Word

*"Every word of God proves true." — **Proverbs 30:5a***

Scripture: Proverbs 30:5

Visual Aid: Picture story of Pansy

Handouts: Activity sheets

Advance Preparations: Copy enough activity sheets for each child to have one and have them ready to hand out. Also make enough copies of the Pansy story page (page 25) for yourself and each child. Fold the page in half the long way so that page 1 is at the bottom right corner. Fold again the other way. The story will then have pages 1 through 4 in order. Be ready to use the folder with the children as you tell the story. (If your children are old enough and you have time, let them fold their own with your guidance.)

The Sermon:
We talked about the turtle and his shells. They are shelter for him. We have shelter, too, if we love and obey Jesus. He comes to us and lives with us. One of the important ways we have his shelter (protection) is by obeying what he has said.

Today I want to tell you a true story about a little dog whose name was Pansy. This is a true story:

* Page 1. Pansy lived with a family of six children. Pansy and the children had a lot of fun together. But this family lived in a town that had a rule about dogs. No dog was allowed to be loose. A dog could be sent to dog jail and its family had to pay a fine if a dog was caught running loose. So Pansy stayed in the house, or if she was out, she was tied in the backyard. But the children thought Pansy should have a doghouse. If it should rain or get cold, they wanted her to have shelter. So Dad bought a doghouse from a neighbor who had just about anything you could want stored in his backyard.

Page 2. Pansy liked her doghouse. She could get a better look at the world from the top.

Page 3. But Pansy would not go inside her house. She knew how. She knew she was supposed to, but the only time she would was when someone pointed and yelled at her. She would stick her tail between her legs and crawl around on her belly first. She acted as though she was being punished. As soon as no one was looking, she ran out of her house.

Page 4. If Pansy had done as she was told, she would have had shelter.

And so it is with us. If we'll do as we're told, we'll have shelter, too. Now I know you have houses for shelter, but I'm talking about another kind of shelter, shelter from the bad things that can happen to us, like accidents, illness, hurt feelings, and problems of all kinds. Some of these bad things would never happen, we'd be sheltered from them, if we would do as we're told. When Mom and Dad make you obey the rules, do you think they're mean? Do you think that they are punishing you, like Pansy did? Not so! Mom and Dad make rules for your own good because they care for your happiness. If Mom says, "Brush your teeth," she is trying to shelter you from cavities in your teeth and from toothache. If you are told to eat your vegetables or drink your milk, you are being sheltered from a weak and sickly body.

It is the same with us all when we know what Jesus has taught. We should be careful to obey him because he knows what will make us happy and he knows what will cause us harm.

Let's see what the Bible says: "Every word of God proves true; he is a shield to those who take refuge in him" (Proverbs 30:5).

This is telling us that God's word is true. In God and in his word we have protection and shelter.

It is important to come to Sunday school and church and learn what Jesus says. It is important to obey him.

*Use visual aid

The Penguin: Working Together

"... be united in the same mind and the same purpose." — 1 Corinthians 1:10b

Scripture: 1 Corinthians 1:10b; see also Galatians 5:13-15

Visual Aid: Picture of the penguin

Handouts: Activity sheets

Advance Preparations: Copy enough activity sheets for each child to have one and have them ready to hand out. Copy and color the picture of the penguin to use as a visual aid as you give the lesson. Or if you prefer, check with your library for pictures to show your children.

The Sermon:

Some birds and animals who are alike work together for the good of their group. Penguins do. They live many miles south of here where there is mostly ice and water. * The penguin looks like it is all dressed up in a black suit and white shirt!

Penguins are birds that can't fly. Their wings are more like flippers. They can dive in water and swim very well, but on land they are very awkward. One kind of penguin lays on its stomach and slides along like a sled, using its flippers like oars.

These birds are very sociable. That means that they like to stay in groups. They even make their nests and hatch their babies in groups. Most Mom and Dad penguins both work to care for the baby penguin, but when the babies are a little older, they are left in a nursery of about twenty other babies. Three or four older birds act as baby-sitters. Then Mom and Dad Penguin go fishing and share their catch with the group.

They all work together. They seem to know and agree on what needs to be done and how and who will do it. Penguins are alike and work together for the good of the whole group.

We can learn something from penguins. The Bible says in 1 Corinthians 1:10b: "... be united in the same mind and the same purpose." We are part of a group of people who are mostly alike. We live in the same community, speak the same language, and come to the same church. We believe that Jesus is Lord and should be obeyed. We ought to work and play well together. Do we? Do we try hard to get along with others? Do we try to help them? Love them? Forgive them? It might even mean letting someone else have their way. Let's try.

*Use visual aid

The Rhinoceros And The Tickbird:
Working Together Though Not Alike

"For we are God's servants, working together...." — 1 Corinthians 3:9a

Scripture: 1 Corinthians 3:9a; see also Galatians 3:26-28

Visual Aid: Picture of the rhinoceros

Handouts: Activity sheets

Advance Preparations: Copy enough activity sheets for each child to have one and have them ready to hand out. Copy and color the picture of the rhinoceros to use as a visual aid as you give the lesson. Or if you prefer, check with your library for pictures to show your children.

The Sermon:
Do you remember when we talked about penguins? What do you remember about them? They are alike and they work together for the good of all.

Today we'll talk about two animals that are not at all alike. Yet they are able to work together for their own good. * The rhinoceros is very big and kind of ugly. It lives in Africa and Asia. Its head is big and its chest, legs, bones, and muscles are all big. Some weigh as much as 2,000 pounds. Its skin is thick and it has a big horn right in the middle of its forehead. It has very poor eyesight. That's probably because that horn is in the way. A rhinoceros is said to have a bad temper and can be very dangerous. It does not eat meat, but it will charge and trample and toss an enemy with that big horn. It bites with its big teeth.

The rhinoceros doesn't have any friends, but it does have a partner. Its partner is the tickbird. The tickbird hangs onto the rhinoceros with strong claws and eats ticks that stick in the rhinoceros' skin. The bird gets plenty to eat and, in exchange, it warns its partner by making a great commotion if danger is near, because the rhinoceros cannot see well.

These two are not alike, yet they work together for their own good. 1 Corinthians 3:9 says: "For we are God's servants, working together...." This should be easy when people are all alike, but we must learn to work together even if we are not alike, and God's people are not all alike. Some call themselves by different names (Methodist, Lutheran, Baptist, and so on). Some have very different ways of worship, but it is the same God and Lord Jesus we all love and worship. If we all work together we can accomplish much good, like providing food for the hungry or help for people in floods or tornadoes, or perhaps by participating in community Bible school, community choirs, or community prayer days. We all benefit from working together.

The Bible says in Galatians 3:26-28 that when people love Christ Jesus, they are all children of God. It doesn't matter how different each one is.

If we can, we also must try to work with people who do not know Jesus as their Lord, for our own good, for world peace, for freedom and help for people all around the world, no matter how different they might be.

The tickbird does not want to be a rhinoceros. It remains a tickbird. In the same way, God's people remain Christians. But perhaps by showing love and care and a willingness to work with others, people who are not Christians will see something good and want to know Jesus, too. Yes, working together with others is the best way.

*Use visual aid

The Opossum: Playing Dead To Sin

"... consider yourselves dead to sin and alive to God in Christ Jesus." — Romans 6:11b

Scripture: Romans 6:11

Visual Aid: Picture of the opossum

Handouts: Activity sheets

Advance Preparations: Copy enough activity sheets for each child to have one and have them ready to hand out. Copy and color the picture of the opossum to use as a visual aid as you give the lesson. Or if you prefer, check with your library for pictures to show your children.

The Sermon:
Today I want to talk about a little animal called an opossum. * It grows to be fifteen to twenty inches long, but it has a tail that is another nine or ten inches long. Its tail helps it to climb trees, and it uses it to hang from branches sometimes. This is the only animal in North America that carries its babies in a pouch when they are first born, like a kangaroo. When the babies are about as big as a small mouse, they begin to ride around on their mother's back.

Have you ever "played 'possum"? Do you know how? You play 'possum by pretending to be asleep when you really are not. Lay your head back, close your eyes, don't move, and breathe slowly. That is "playing 'possum." Maybe if you play 'possum, Dad or Mom will carry you into the house after a long trip in the car.

We call this game playing 'possum because the animal, the opossum, really does do this, but actually it is playing dead. When it is in danger from another animal, such as a coyote, the opossum falls over, sticks its legs out, and opens its mouth with teeth showing. It closes its eyes or sometimes leaves them open and they film over. It hardly even breathes. It looks dead. Since most animals want to catch their dinner alive and have fresh meat, they are fooled into thinking that the opossum is dead and they won't touch it. After the danger is over, the opossum comes back to life and runs away.

Some people think opossums are a little stupid, but I think they are smart. You and I would be smart too if we would learn from the opossum to "play dead" in our minds and hearts when things happen that cause us to want to do something wrong. You see, something that is dead cannot do anything wrong. If we get the idea to lie, cheat, steal, hurt someone, or do other wrong things, we should "play dead" to that wrong thing, and then we cannot do it. The Bible says this very thing in Romans 6:11: "So you also must consider yourselves dead to sin and alive to God in Christ Jesus." We are dead to wrong, hurtful things *but* alive to good, happy things found in Christ Jesus.

*Use visual aid

The Squirrel: Gathering Treasures

"... store up for yourselves treasures in heaven." — Matthew 6:20a

Scripture: Matthew 6:19-21

Visual Aid: Picture of the squirrel

Handouts: Activity sheet

Advance Preparations: Copy enough activity sheets for each child to have one and have them ready to hand out. Copy and color the picture of the squirrel to use as a visual aid as you give the lesson. Or if you prefer, check with your library for pictures to show your children.

The Sermon:

Have you ever seen a squirrel? They are fun to watch. They run here and there and look very busy. A tree squirrel climbs trees and balances itself very well on limbs. Its long bushy tail helps. Squirrels eat seeds, nuts, and fruits. Sometimes they bury a nut and forget to come back for it. What do you think happens then? It grows and becomes another nut tree.

Squirrels plan ahead and store up food for the time when food might be hard to find. We can learn from squirrels to plan ahead.

Squirrels work hard to gather food to keep alive. People have to work hard, too, but we need to remember that we shouldn't be working just to get rich and to own stuff. Money, houses, land, jewelry, and such things are not lasting. They can be stolen, destroyed by fire or flood perhaps, or lose value, and at the best they last only a few years while we live. Jesus said something about this in Matthew 6:19-20: "Do not store up for yourselves treasures on earth, where moth and rust consume and where thieves break in and steal; but store up for yourselves treasures in heaven."

Treasures in heaven are earned when we love and obey Jesus and when we love and help others. If you start now, as young as you are, just think what a great amount of treasure you'll have when one day you reach heaven!

But, you know, there are treasures on earth, too, that have nothing to do with owning stuff. The best things in life, such as love, joy, peace, happiness, and satisfaction, are real treasures and come to us here on earth if we do love and obey Jesus, and love and help others.

*Use visual aid

The Turtle

Color the turtle brown or grey with yellow spots and orange eyes.

Turtles

There are many kinds of turtles. One that lives in many areas is a box turtle. It lives on land but likes to be near water.

Turtles don't have teeth, but they have a strong horny bill which can tear their food. It might be insects, worms, snails, fruit, or berries.

Turtles have two shells, a round one and a bottom flat one. Their head, legs, and tail stick out between the two shells. When frightened, the box turtle will pull his head, tail, and legs in, then shut tight the bottom shell against the top. With this good protection, turtles may live to be very old.

We have homes for shelter. Yet there is more for God's people. The Bible says, "God is our refuge [shelter] and strength, a very present help in trouble" (Psalm 46:1). It also says that if we love and obey Jesus he will come and live with us. He shelters and protects us from harm by teaching us how to live our lives; he hears our prayers and helps.

It's up to us to trust him.

This turtle is closing its shell. When it comes out it will be hungry. Help it find the worms on this page. How many are there? _____

Find the words in the list. They go to the right or down.

```
L O V E X X I B T L
P E O P L E N I A E
I X P R A Y S L I G
N T W O S H E L L S
H U O T X X C A O J
O R R E A T T N B E
R T M C X X S D E S
N L S T O B E Y R U
Y E S H E L T E R S
B O X T R O U B L E
F R U I T S N A I L
```

Land	**Tail**	**Fruit**	**Pray**
Box	**Horny**	**Snail**	**Shelter**
Turtle	**Bill**	**People**	**In**
Two	**Eat**	**Trouble**	**Jesus**
Shells	**Insects**	**Love**	**Legs**
Protect	**Worms**	**Obey**	

Across

1. A kind of turtle b_____.
2. Something turtles eat s_____.
3. Something pulled into shelter by turtle l_____.
4. God's people can say, "God is our s_____.
5. Jesus asks us to l_____ and obey him.

Down

a. Something turtles eat _____.
b. Something turtles use to tear food _____.
c. A turtle has two _____ for protection.
d. Something pulled into shelter by turtle _____.
e. Jesus lives with those who love and _____ him.

12

The Dog

Color Pansy

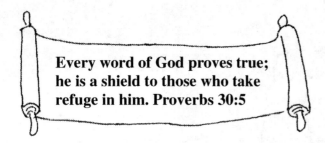

Every word of God proves true; he is a shield to those who take refuge in him. Proverbs 30:5

Read the Bible verse. Then choose the right word from the list to fill in the blanks.

problems
protection
true
shelter
happy
obey

Another word for shield is _ _ _ _ _ _ _ _ _ _.
Another word for refuge is _ _ _ _ _ _ _.
God's word is _ _ _ _.
If we will _ _ _ _ what God's word teaches, we will be sheltered from all kinds of _ _ _ _ _ _ _ _.
We will have _ _ _ _ _ lives in God's care.

Why would Mom or Dad say this? Draw a line to match the sentence with the right answer.

Shut the door.	Your body needs the vitamins.
Don't tease the cat.	So cavities won't form.
Drink your milk.	Cleanliness is healthy.
Eat your vegetables.	Learn all you can for a better future.
Brush your teeth.	Washing kills germs that make you sick.
Do your homework.	Cold air comes in.
Go to bed.	You might get scratched.
Take your shower.	Milk builds strong bones.
Clean your room.	Keeping warm helps you stay well.
Say you're sorry.	Others will want cookies, too.
Don't eat candy now.	Your body needs rest to grow.
Wear a hat.	Don't spread germs.
Wash your hands before lunch.	Learn to get along; you'll want friends.
Take only two cookies.	It might spoil your dinner.
Help your sister.	Don't bring mud into the house.
Wipe your feet.	You don't want to get hit.
Cover your mouth when you cough.	If you should fall, you are protected.
Wipe your nose.	You work and rest better in a clean room.
Look for cars before crossing.	Don't spread germs.
Wear a helmet when you ride your bike.	A family helps each other.

The Penguin

Color the penguin's head, bill, flippers, and back black. The front is white, and a white patch is on the bill. The eyes are yellow; feet are orange.

Connect The Dots.

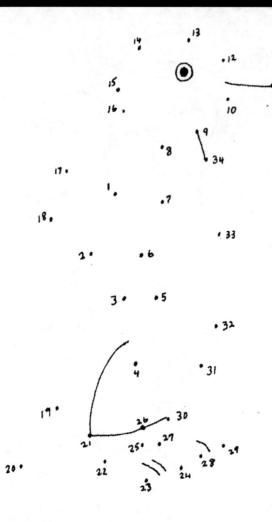

**Fill in the blanks using words
from the story about penguins.**

Penguins are birds that cannot _ _ _.
They live in _ _ _ _ _ _ _ _ _ _.
Penguins can _ _ _ _ and _ _ _ _ very well.
Older penguins are _ _ _ _ - _ _ _ _ _ _ _.
They take care of _ _ _ _ penguins while
Mom and Dad Penguin catch _ _ _ _ to feed all.
Penguins work _ _ _ _ _ _ _ _.
God's people must _ _ _ _ together.
The Bible says that we should
_ _ _ _ _ one another because
we love each other.

Penguins

Penguins are a kind of bird that lives many miles south of here in Antarctica, a place of ice and water. Penguins don't fly, but they dive and swim well. Out of the water, they waddle awkwardly as they walk. Some lay on their stomachs and slide around, using flippers as oars.

Most Mom and Dad penguins take turns hatching and caring for the eggs and new chicks, but as soon as the babies are partly grown, they are placed in a nursery of twenty or so other young penguins. A few old birds are baby-sitters while the adults go fishing for food for all. Penguins work well together. It's easy to work in a group where all are alike.

God's people must work together for the good of one another. In the Bible (Galatians 5:13-15) we learn that we should serve, help, and care for one another, because we love each other.

See the list for words that go down or to the right.

L	S	E	R	V	E	S	W	I	M
O	P	E	N	G	U	I	N	S	D
V	G	G	E	R	F	T	S	H	I
E	O	G	W	O	L	T	W	X	V
X	W	S	O	U	Y	E	I	C	E
E	N	X	R	P	X	R	M	A	A
A	L	I	K	E	X	S	X	N	L
T	T	O	G	E	T	H	E	R	L
F	I	S	H	G	R	O	W	N	X

Penguins	**Sitters**
Group	**Eat**
Alike	**Fish**
Fly	**Can**
Dive	**Work**
Swim (twice)	**Together**
Ice	**All**
New	**Love**
Eggs	**Serve**
Grown	

16

The Rhinoceros And The Tickbird

First outline the rhinoceros with black, then lightly color with black or brown; the bird is black.

Rhinoceros and Tickbird

The rhinoceros lives in Asia and Africa close to water. It is said to have a terrible temper, and is big, strong, and dangerous. Yet it has a partner. The partner is a small bird that rides on the back of the rhinoceros. It holds on with strong claws and uses its bill like a spear to eat the ticks that live in the rhinoceros' hide. The horn in the middle of a rhinoceros' head keeps it from seeing well, so in exchange for food the tickbird warns its partner of danger. The rhinoceros and the tickbird are not alike at all, yet they work together for their own good. The Bible says, "For we are God's servants working together...." We can learn from these two animals. We must learn to work together, even when we are not all alike, for our own good.

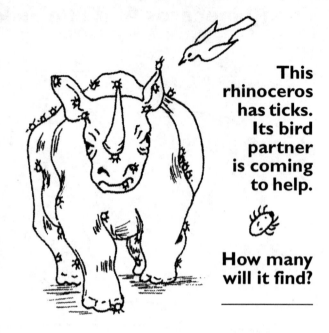

This rhinoceros has ticks. Its bird partner is coming to help.

How many will it find?

_____

servants | bird
work | alike
ticks | together
partners | people
horn | working

Use words from the list to fill in the blanks AND the squares.

1. The rhinoceros has a _ _ _ _ for a partner.

2. The rhinoceros has a _ _ _ _ in the middle of its head that keeps it from seeing well.

3. The bird and rhinoceros are not at all

   _ _ _ _ _.

4. They are _ _ _ _ _ _ _ _ _.

5. They work _ _ _ _ _ _ _ _.

6. The bird eats _ _ _ _ _ from the hide of a rhinoceros. In exchange for the food, the bird warns the rhinoceros of danger.

7 & 8. God's _ _ _ _ _ _ should _ _ _ _ together even when they are not alike.

9 & 10. The Bible says we are _ _ _ _ _ _ _ together as God's _ _ _ _ _ _ _ _ _.

18

The Opossum

Color the opossum grey with a very light grey face.

Opossums

The opossum is a little animal that looks something like a giant rat, because it has a long, scaly tail. Opossums grow to fifteen or twenty inches with a tail that is another nine or ten inches long. They climb trees and use their tails for balance and to hang from limbs. It is the only animal in North America that carries its babies in a pouch like a kangaroo. When the babies are about as big as a small mouse, they begin to ride around on their mother's back. Opossums come out mostly at night. They eat insects, snakes, dead animals, grains, and fruit. An opossum doesn't have any way to defend itself, so it has learned to "play dead." It hopes to escape notice by falling over with its mouth open and teeth showing. Its eyes close or film over and it barely breathes. It does this because most animals that hunt want to catch their dinner alive and won't eat already dead meat. When danger is over, it comes to life and then escapes.

We can learn something from the opossum. When we are tempted to do something wrong, we can "play dead" to the thing that is wrong and not do it. The Bible says: "So you also must consider yourselves dead to sin and alive to God in Christ Jesus" (Romans 6:11).

Unscramble the words and fill in the blanks.

An _____ is a little animal with a
ssoopmu

long, scaly _____. Mother
ilat

opossums carry their _____ in
bbaies

_____. When they are old
sehcuop

enough, they ride on her back. If an

opossum is in _____, it falls
gerdan

down and _____ dead. When the
lpyas

danger is gone, it gets up and

_____. The Bible says, "So
csepsea

_____ must consider yourselves
uoy

_____ to _____ and
aedd   sni

_____ to God in Christ Jesus"
veial

(Romans 6:11).

Read the list of things to do. If it is wrong, draw a line to the opossum that is playing dead. If it would please Jesus, draw a line to the "alive" opossum.

take candy from the store without paying for it

help do the dishes

help Sister with homework

copy another person's answers

tell Brother that he is dumb

laugh when a boy at school falls down

break a dish, tell Mom you didn't

try taking drugs

help Grandma sweep the floor

push others to be first in line

The Squirrel

Color the squirrel grey or reddish brown.

Squirrels

A tree squirrel is grey or reddish brown. Its long bushy tail helps the squirrel to balance as it leaps from branch to branch. The tail is also a warm blanket to wrap up in on cold nights. Usually tree squirrels live in hollow trunks or limbs, but sometimes they build nests of leaves and twigs. Squirrels eat seeds, nuts, and fruits. Often they bury nuts as they gather and store food for the winter. (Sometimes these nuts are forgotten and they grow to become trees.) Squirrels plan ahead for their winter when food will be hard to find.

God expects his people to be wise and plan ahead, too. Yet many times God's people forget that no one can count on what they get and own to bring happiness now or in the future. Money, land, houses, or other things do not last. Jesus said, "Store up for yourselves treasures in heaven" (Matthew 6:20a).

Treasures in heaven are gotten when we love and obey Jesus, and when we love and help others.

Help the squirrel find nuts, but don't cross any lines.

How many nuts can the squirrel take home?

_____

How many nuts must he leave behind?

_____

Find the words that are in the list. They go to the right or down.

```
G E N T L E P R A I S E T O
W I S E O T H E R S E U A W
N A G X V P L A N H E P I N
U L O V E O B E Y A D K L N
T L D T R E E F O R G I V E
R I C H E S T O R E X N D S
H E A V E N B U S H Y D O T
S Q U I R R E L A H E A D S
```

Store	Kind	Love	Own
Up	Gentle	Others	Bushy
Riches	Forgive	Wise	Tail
In	Share	Plan	Nests
Heaven	Praise	Ahead	Tree
Do	Love	All	Nut
Obey	God	Squirrel	Seed

These boys and girls were helpful. Which sentence is true if they are storing treasures in heaven? Put a line under that sentence.

Jane watched little Joe so that Joe's mother could visit Grandpa in the nursing home.

1. Jane asked for $1 an hour.

2. Jane would not take pay.

Jerry sings in the children's choir at church.

1. Jerry's mother has to make him.

2. Jerry likes to praise God with songs.

Mary did supper dishes for Mother, who was very tired.

1. Mary offered to do them.

2. Mary's mother had to beg for help.

ANSWER KEYS

Pages 12, 14, 16

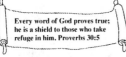

Turtles

There are many kinds of turtles. One that lives in many areas is a box turtle. It lives on land but likes to be near water.

Turtles don't have teeth, but they have a strong horny bill which can tear their food. It might be insects, worms, snails, fruit, or berries.

Turtles have two shells, a round one and a bottom flat one. Their head, legs, and tail stick out between the two shells. When frightened, the box turtle will pull his head, tail, and legs in, then shut tight the bottom shell against the top. With this good protection, turtles may live to be very old.

We have homes for shelter. Yet there is more for God's people. The Bible says, "God is our refuge [shelter] and strength, a very present help in trouble" (Psalm 46:1). It also says that if we love and obey Jesus he will come and live with us. He shelters and protects us from harm by teaching us how to live our lives; he hears our prayers and helps.

It's up to us to trust him.

This turtle is closing its shell. When it comes out it will be hungry. Help it find the worms on this page. How many are there? __26__

Find the words in the list. They go to the right or down.

L	O	V	E	X	X		I	B	T	L	E
P	E	O	P	L	E		N	I	A	E	G
I	X	P	R	A	Y		S	L	I	G	S
N	H	U	T	W	O	S	H	E	L	L	
H	O	R	O	T	X	X	C	A	O	J	E
O	R	T	R	M	E	A	T	N	B	E	S
R	N	L	M	C	X	X	X	D	E	B	U
N	Y	E	S	T	O	B	E	Y			
		S	H	E	L	T	E	R			
B	O	X	T	R	O	U	B	L	E		
F	R	U	I	T	S	N	A	I	L		

Land	Tail	Fruit	Pray
Box	Horny	Snail	Shelter
Turtle	Bill	People	In
Two	Eat	Trouble	Jesus
Shells	Insects	Love	Legs
Protect	Worms	Obey	

Crossword grid with answers:

Across
1. A kind of turtle b __ox__.
2. Something turtles eat s __nail__.
3. Something pulled into shelter by turtle l __egs__.
4. God's people can say, "God is our s __helter__.
5. Jesus asks us to l __ove__ and obey him.

Down
a. Something turtles eat __worm__.
b. Something turtles use to tear food __bill__.
c. A turtle has two __shells__ for protection.
d. Something pulled into shelter by turtle __tail__.
e. Jesus lives with those who love and __obey__ him.

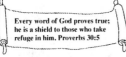

Every word of God proves true; he is a shield to those who take refuge in him. Proverbs 30:5

Read the Bible verse. Then choose the right word from the list to fill in the blanks.

problems
protection
true
shelter
happy
obey

Another word for shield is p r o t e c t i o n.
Another word for refuge is s h e l t e r.
God's word is t r u e.
If we will o b e y what God's word teaches, we will be sheltered from all kinds of p r o b l e m s.
We will have h a p p y lives in God's care.

Why would Mom or Dad say this? Draw a line to match the sentence with the right answer.

Shut the door.	Your body needs the vitamins.
Don't tease the cat.	So cavities won't form.
Drink your milk.	Cleanliness is healthy.
Eat your vegetables.	Learn all you can for a better future.
Brush your teeth.	Washing kills germs that make you sick.
Do your homework.	Cold air comes in.
Go to bed.	You might get scratched.
Take your shower.	Milk builds strong bones.
Clean your room.	Keeping warm helps you stay well.
Say you're sorry.	Others will want cookies, too.
Don't eat candy now.	Your body needs rest to grow.
Wear a hat.	Don't spread germs.
Wash your hands before lunch.	Learn to get along; you'll want friends.
Take only two cookies.	It might spoil your dinner.
Help your sister.	Don't bring mud into the house.
Wipe your feet.	You don't want to get hit.
Cover your mouth when you cough.	If you should fall, you are protected.
Wipe your nose.	You work and rest better in a clean room.
Look for cars before crossing.	Don't spread germs.
Wear a helmet when you ride your bike.	A family helps each other.

Connect The Dots.

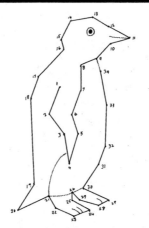

Fill in the blanks using words from the story about penguins.

Penguins are birds that cannot f l y.
They live in A n t a r c t i c a.
Penguins can s w i m and d i v e very well.
Older penguins are b a b y - s i t t e r s.
They take care of b a b y penguins while
Mom and Dad Penguin catch f i s h to feed all.
Penguins work t o g e t h e r.
God's people must w o r k together.
The Bible says that we should
s e r v e one another because
we love each other.

Penguins

Penguins are a kind of bird that lives many miles south of here in Antarctica, a place of ice and water. Penguins don't fly, but they dive and swim well. Out of the water, they waddle awkwardly as they walk. Some lay on their stomachs and slide around, using flippers as oars.

Most Mom and Dad penguins take turns hatching and caring for the eggs and new chicks, but as soon as the babies are partly grown, they are placed in a nursery of twenty or so other young penguins. A few old birds are baby-sitters while the adults go fishing for food for all. Penguins work well together. It's easy to work in a group where all are alike.

God's people must work together for the good of one another. In the Bible (Galatians 5:13-15) we learn that we should serve, help, and care for one another, because we love each other.

See the list for words that go down or to the right.

L	S	E	R	V	E	S	W	I	M
O	P	E	N	G	U	I	N	S	D
V	G	G	E	R	F	T	S	H	I
E	O	G	W	O	L	T	M	W	X
X	W	S	O	U	Y	E	I	C	E
E	N	X	R	P	X	R	M	A	A
A	L	I	K	E	X	S	X	N	L
T	O	G	E	T	H	E	R	L	
F	I	S	H	G	R	O	W	N	X

Penguins	Sitters
Group	Eat
Alike	Fish
Fly	Can
Dive	Work
Swim (twice)	Together
Ice	All
New	Love
Eggs	Serve
Grown	

ANSWER KEYS

Pages 18, 20, 22

Rhinoceros and Tickbird

The rhinoceros lives in Asia and Africa close to water. It is said to have a terrible temper, and is big, strong, and dangerous. Yet it has a partner. The partner is a small bird that rides on the back of the rhinoceros. It holds on with strong claws and uses its bill like a spear to eat the ticks that live in the rhinoceros' hide. The horn in the middle of a rhinoceros' head keeps it from seeing well, so in exchange for food the tickbird warns its partner of danger. The rhinoceros and the tickbird are not alike at all, yet they work together for their own good. The Bible says, "For we are God's servants working together...." We can learn from these two animals. We must learn to work together, even when we are not all alike, for our own good.

This rhinoceros has ticks. Its bird partner is coming to help.

How many will it find?
29

servants
work
ticks
partners
horn

bird
alike
together
people
working

Use words from the list to fill in the blanks AND the squares.

1. The rhinoceros has a b i r d for a partner.
2. The rhinoceros has a h o r n in the middle of its head that keeps it from seeing well.
3. The bird and rhinoceros are not at all a l i k e.
4. They are p a r t n e r s.
5. They work t o g e t h e r.
6. The bird eats t i c k s from the hide of a rhinoceros. In exchange for the food, the bird warns the rhinoceros of danger.
7 & 8. God's p e o p l e should w o r k together even when they are not alike.
9 & 10. The Bible says we are w o r k i n g together as God's s e r v a n t s.

Opossums

The opossum is a little animal that looks something like a giant rat, because it has a long, scaly tail. Opossums grow to fifteen or twenty inches with a tail that is another nine or ten inches long. They climb trees and use their tails for balance and to hang from limbs. It is the only animal in North America that carries its babies in a pouch like a kangaroo. When the babies are about as big as a small mouse, they begin to ride around on their mother's back. Opossums come out mostly at night. They eat insects, snakes, dead animals, grains, and fruit. An opossum doesn't have any way to defend itself, so it has learned to "play dead." It hopes to escape notice by falling over with its mouth open and teeth showing. Its eyes close or film over and it barely breathes. It does this because most animals that hunt want to catch their dinner alive and won't eat already dead meat. When danger is over, it comes to life and then escapes.

We can learn something from the opossum. When we are tempted to do something wrong, we can "play dead" to the thing that is wrong and not do it. The Bible says: "So you also must consider yourselves dead to sin and alive to God in Christ Jesus" (Romans 6:11).

Unscramble the words and fill in the blanks.

An __opossum__ is a little animal with a
ssoopmu
long, scaly __tail__. Mother
ilat
opossums carry their __babies__ in
bbaies
__pouches__. When they are old
sehcuop
enough, they ride on her back. If an
opossum is in __danger__, it falls
gerdan
down and __plays__ dead. When the
lpyas
danger is gone, it gets up and
__escapes__. The Bible says, "So
csepsea
__you__ must consider yourselves
uoy
__dead__ to __sin__ and
aedd   sni
__alive__ to God in Christ Jesus"
veial
(Romans 6:11).

Read the list of things to do. If it is wrong, draw a line to the opossum that is playing dead. If it would please Jesus, draw a line to the "alive" opossum.

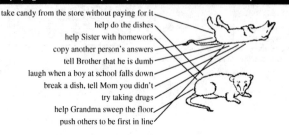

take candy from the store without paying for it
help do the dishes
help Sister with homework
copy another person's answers
tell Brother that he is dumb
laugh when a boy at school falls down
break a dish, tell Mom you didn't
try taking drugs
help Grandma sweep the floor
push others to be first in line

Squirrels

A tree squirrel is grey or reddish brown. Its long bushy tail helps the squirrel to balance as it leaps from branch to branch. The tail is also a warm blanket to wrap up in on cold nights. Usually tree squirrels live in hollow trunks or limbs, but sometimes they build nests of leaves and twigs. Squirrels eat seeds, nuts, and fruits. Often they bury nuts as they gather and store food for the winter. (Sometimes these nuts are forgotten and they grow to become trees.) Squirrels plan ahead for their winter when food will be hard to find.

God expects his people to be wise and plan ahead, too. Yet many times God's people forget that no one can count on what they get and own to bring happiness now or in the future. Money, land, houses, or other things do not last. Jesus said, "Store up for yourselves treasures in heaven" (Matthew 6:20a).

Treasures in heaven are gotten when we love and obey Jesus, and when we love and help others.

Find the words that are in the list. They go to the right or down.

G E N T L E P R A I S E T O
W I S E O T H E R S E U A W
N A G X V P L A N H E P I N
U L O V E O B E Y A D K L N
T L D T R E E F O R G I V E
R I C H E S T O R E X N D S
H E A V E N B U S H Y D O T
S Q U I R R E L A H E A D S

Store   Kind   Love   Own
Up   Gentle   Others   Bushy
Riches   Forgive   Wise   Tail
In   Share   Plan   Nests
Heaven   Praise   Ahead   Tree
Do   Love   All   Nut
Obey   God   Squirrel Seed

Help the squirrel find nuts, but don't cross any lines.

How many nuts can the squirrel take home?
9

How many nuts must he leave behind?
4

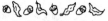

These boys and girls were helpful. Which sentence is true if they are storing treasures in heaven? Put a line under that sentence.

Jane watched little Joe so that Joe's mother could visit Grandpa in the nursing home.
1. Jane asked for $1 an hour.
2. Jane would not take pay.

Jerry sings in the children's choir at church.
1. Jerry's mother has to make him.
2. Jerry likes to praise God with songs.

Mary did supper dishes for Mother, who was very tired.
1. Mary offered to do them.
2. Mary's mother had to beg for help.

If she would obey, she'd have shelter.

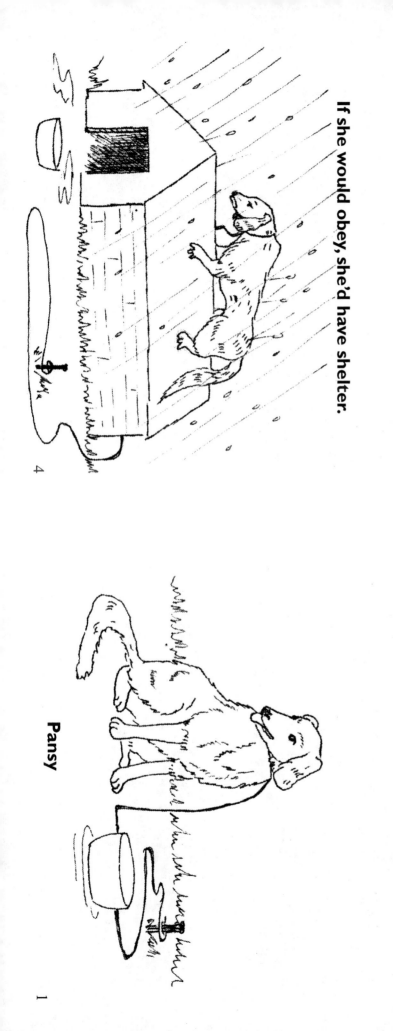

4

But she wouldn't go in it.

3

Pansy

1

Pansy liked to sit on her doghouse.

2

PANSY